# THE JEWISH HOLOCAUSTS
# WHY? WHY GOD? WHY?

by

ROBERT EUCLIDE POUDRIER

All right reserved. No part of this book may be reproduced or transmitted in any form without written permission from the publisher or author, except for inclusion of brief quotations in reviews, or for individual personal use.

Copyright © 2001 by Robert E. Poudrier.

ISBN : 0-615-11960-3

OTHER PUBLICATIONS BY AUTHOR

"Adventures in the Christian Life"........5,000 copies sold

"My Servant Job".......Sreenplay

Writer's Press
15417 Chaparral Street
Victorville, CA 92394
(760) 241 - 3927
REPoudrier@juno.com

# FORWARD

By Dr. Paul Bianchini ; Th.D

My prayer is that everyone who reads this book understands that life, without the Lamb of God Yeshua, is useless. God made a way for man to live in liberty. He created man and that man fell in sin and needed a way out. God provided a way out through his Ancient Covenanted peoples - The Jews, by providing a Messiah through them.

Robert points this all out well and that people are living under the blessing or the curse. Both the blessing and/or the curse is to the Jew first and then to the gentile. As a believer in Yeshua, the Jewish Messiah and a son of Holocaust survivors, I pray that all peoples see this in the spiritual context and enlightenment that the words display for ones own examination and introspection.

Deepest appreciation is expressed to my daughter, Peggy Lind Poudrier-Crow. Peggy worked tirelessly on typing, editing, proofreading, etc. Also to Pastor Dan Barbour, Vince Onken, Mary Jo Swanson and especially to Frank Stooksbury for advice, review and proofreading. Special thanks to Dr. Paul Bianchini, President and Founder of The Bible Institute of Jerusalem, for taking the time to review this manuscript and for his advise.

## CONTENTS

| CHAPTER | | PAGE |
|---|---|---|
| I | Why? Why God? Why? | 1 |
| II | World Wide Execution of Jews | 10 |
| III | The Law | 16 |
| IV | Good Laws | 25 |
| V | Is Yeshua the Messiah? | 48 |
| VI | Who Killed Yeshua? | 54 |
| VII | 1st or 2nd Degree Murder | 76 |
| VIII | Melchizedek | 83 |
| IX | The King is Coming | 96 |
| X | What About the Gentiles | 101 |

# The Jewish Holocausts

## Chapter I
## Why? Why God? Why?

The taxi arrived at our pre-arranged apartment in Jerusalem late Saturday afternoon after Shabbat. We removed all our large traveling bags from the top and back of the taxi and hauled them up the first floor to our comfortably furnished flat.

This was our new home for the next eight months. We loved it. We were located at No. 8 Haran St., Apt. #4. The main cross streets, one block away, were Karim Kayemet and Usshishkin. Our neighborhood was French Jewish Orthodox. We were a short walking distance to Ben Yehuda St., the center of activity with many street cafes, restaurants, and shops. Street musicians, clowns and beggars were in abundance setting the atmosphere. This became a fun place to come and relax.

Meyer's Cafe was across the street from the corner of our house. The coffee and croissants were the best in Jerusalem. We slowly made friends with a few of the daily customers.

We came to Israel to specifically get to know the Jewish people. We wanted to understand their minds and know their thinking. We found very soon that the Jewish people were really anti-Yeshua Messiah (Jesus as the Christ).

Why? All of my life since I received Jesus the Christ as my Savior, my Messiah, the Messiah of Israel, I have prayed for Jerusalem and the Jewish people. And, without even knowing them I came to love them. Now Marion and I came to Israel, not to see the sights but to get to know the people.

In the many conversations we were having with the Jewish people the most common questions were about the Holocaust.

This Holocaust is where over 6 million Jews were killed during World War II by, so called, Christians. Germany was considered a Christian nation, partly Protestant and partly Roman Catholic.

The common answer from Jewish survivors is, "We will not forget! We will never forgive!"

They would often remind us of the slaughter of Jews in the city of Jerusalem around 1,100 A.D. at the hands of the Roman Catholic Pope, who ordered the Crusades and commanded the German emperor to send the first army of Crusaders to free the Holy Land from the Muslims.

And, yes, they remember by the careful and meticulous teaching from their families and Rabbis, the atrocities committed against the Jewish people over the centuries.

All through the 1200 years of the Dark Ages millions of Jews were killed and their properties confiscated. They were imprisoned, tortured, humiliated and forced to flee their nations of refuge.

Yes, they remember.

No, they won't forgive.

In Italy, Rome, Spain, France, Germany, England, Ireland, all Roman Catholic Europe and the Middle East, Jews were chased down in the guettos. And after the Protestant movement they were persecuted by the State Churches. Where ever the Jews went they found no rest for the soles of their feet.

During the same 1,200 years of Dark Ages the Ana-baptists, under several different group names, and Jews were persecuted by the Roman Catholic Church under the orders of the Popes.

The Ana-baptists were not a church or an organization. They were believers in Jesus, who converted from the Roman Catholic teachings of salvation by infant baptism at birth, When they came to know the Biblical teachings, they found that salvation was only by receiving Christ as Messiah and Savior. When they made this decision to follow the Messiah and His teachings, the Holy Spirit came into their life and they experienced the new spiritual life they found in a personal relationship with Jesus. Then, they insisted that they be re-baptised to confirm that they were now followers of Jesus Christ. The term "Ana-baptist" means twice baptised.

The Ana-baptists followed the basic teachings of the New Testament, which was the teachings of the Jewish Apostles. These true believers in Christ grew rapidly. They also were hounded by the Roman Catholic Church at the order of the Popes. They were chased down, tortured, killed and their properties confiscated. They scattered all over Europe. They hid in the mountains and in caves, and traveled far to escape their tormentors. They carried the Gospel where ever they went and many received Jesus Christ as their Savior.

It is estimated that during that 1200 years of the dark ages and after, that 25 million fundamental and evangelical Christians, from the body of Christian believers, were murdered and became martyrs. They took on many other names other than Ana-baptists, the Lombards,

Paulicians, Arnoldists, Albigenses, Baptists Waldenses, etc., etc. Today, they are largely the fundamental evangelical Christians. Historical records are available to fully substantiate this. *

In one area of France on a 25-mile road from one town to another the following is recorded. Poles were planted in the ground only a few feet from each other, along the entire 25 miles. Upon the top of the poles were the heads of these "true Christian believers" who would not recant and join the Roman Catholic Church.

The Roman Catholic Church today still recognizes the Pope and the Roman Catholic

---

*The Trail of Blood and listed sources, Ashland Ave. Baptist Church, Lexington, Kentucky. Copyright 1931

teachings as their final authority in all spiritual matters. The Protestants and especially the fundamental evangelical believers place the Bible, Old and New Testament, as the Word of God, and Jesus Christ as their only and final authority in all spiritual matters. And, again, as it was taught by our Jewish apostles.

The Jewish Holocausts are well known by most Jews. However, most Jews know little of the early Jewish Christian believers or of the Gentiles they converted to Christ the Messiah. They grew and spread the Gospel of Jeshua the Messiah all over the World. These "Christians" are the "wheat" in the Christian field and not the "tares" (weeds that look like wheat). The world, for the most part cannot tell the difference. As a result "Christians" are placed in one lump sum.

## Chapter II
## WORLD WIDE EXECUTION OF THE JEWS

God's love for His very own chosen people, all the children of Abraham, is proven in numerous and profound ways. This has been known the world over for many generations except for the last 2,500 years.

The historical records of the killings of the Jews by the Babylonian Empire, Roman Emperors, the Roman Catholic Church and today by Arab fanatical terrorist groups, the Muslims, the Catholic Crusaders, Adolph Hitler in Germany in World War II are also well recorded. Is it strange that the Jews, since the crucifixion of Jesus their Messiah, that they have not found any rest for the soles of their feet? Not on earth or even in Jerusalem? Why?

The murder of hundreds of Jews in 1100 A.D. in Jerusalem at the hands of the Crusaders, who killed all the people seeking refuge in a synagogue.

And the murder of the early Christian Jews by the Roman Emperors is well recorded. It all started at the Cross when the High Priests and the Jewish people shouted to the pro-council, Pilate, "Crucify him, crucify him".

The atrocities against the Jews during the dark ages by the Roman Catholic Church will not be mentioned here in detail but they included murder and genocide throughout

Europe, pillage of Jewish property, expulsion from adopted homelands, false imprisonment, separation of families, stolen Jewish children, etc., etc., etc. In all the countries across Europe the Roman Catholic Church blessed, encouraged, instigated, condoned the extermination action against the Jews. Why? Why? Oh my God, why?

Mr. Schneider and his wife sat in our living room in Jerusalem. She was a survivor of the World War II Holocaust. She spoke of the horrors that befell her and her family. She was the only survivor of her family.

She said, "Don't tell me about God! There is no God! Don't try to tell me there is a God when He would let all the horrible things happen to my mother and father and my brothers and sister. There is no God! There cannot be a God that would let all these things happen. My family were forced, naked, into gas chambers and then their bodies were dragged and dumped into furnaces." The worst part was that she survived to live this heart wrenching experience for the rest of her life.

I had no answer for the Schneiders. But, now my heart was hurting and aching for them as they carried this very heavy burden of hopelessness. They struggled on with life daily but there was no joy, no future and no hope.

The story of the Schneiders can be repeated thousands of times throughout Israel and by Jewish holocaust survivors all over the world. Why? Why Lord? Why?

The Lord God has guided His people so often with great miracles, that the world over could see the very hand of God reaching down to show the Jewish people the way and His purpose for them in the world. He wanted them to be a blessing to all the world.

Zechariah 8:13.
> *"And it shall come to pass that just as you were a curse among the nations, O house of Judah and house of Israel, so I will save you, and you shall be a blessing, do not fear, let your hands be strong."*

Why would such a loving and concerned God allow all these atrocities to happen to the children of Abraham?

I had to find the answer. How can you share the love of God with the Jews and tell them of their Messiah without a totally satisfactory answer for the victims of these inhuman atrocities? Why? Why God? Why?

I took to the Jewish Scriptures for the answers. The Word of God. The Truth. The Jewish Tanach (which is our Old Testament) and the New Testament, written mostly by our Jewish brothers, believers in Yeshua as Messiah.

## Chapter III
## THE LAW

Let's go back a ways to the first five books of the Tanach, The Torah. God commanded Moses to write in the book of Numbers chapter 35. These are the laws concerning murder and manslaughter.

The Lord God establishes here His laws concerning murder and manslaughter. These are God's laws and God always follows His laws. Many nations of the world have established this same law, even in detail. The very first verse credits these laws to God. Remember these laws in detail.

Numbers Chapter 35

*And the Lord spoke to Moses in the*

*plains of Moab by the Jordan across from Jericho, saying: 2."Command the children of Israel that they give the Levites cities to dwell in from the inheritance of their possession, and you shall also give the Levites common-land around the cities. 3. They shall have the cities to dwell in; and their common-land shall be for their cattle, for their herds, and for all their animals. 4. The common-land of the cities which you will give the Levites shall extend from the wall of the city outward a thousand cubits all around. 5. And you shall measure outside the city on the east side two thousand cubits, on the south side two thousand cubits, on the west side two thousand cubits, and on the north side two thousand cubits. The city shall be in the middle. This shall belong to them as common-land for the cities.*

*6. Now among the cities which you will give to the Levites you shall appoint six cities of refuge; to which a manslayer may flee. And to these you shall add forty-two cities. 7. So all the cities you will give to the Levites shall be forty-eight; these you shall give with their common-land. 8. And the cities which you will give shall be from the possession of the children of Israel; from the larger tribe you shall give many, from the smaller you shall give few. Each shall give some of its*

cities to the Levites, in proportion to the inheritance that each receives."
9. Then the Lord spoke to Moses, saying, 10. "Speak to the children of Israel, and say to them: 'When you cross over the Jordan into the land of Canaan, 11. then you shall appoint cities to be cities of refuge for you, that the manslayer who kills any person accidentally may flee there. 12. They shall be cities of refuge for you from the avenger, that the manslayer may not die until he stands before the congregation in judgment. 13. And of the cities which you give, you shall have six cities of refuge. 14. You shall appoint three cities on this side of the Jordan, and three cities you

shall appoint in the land of Canaan, which will be cities of refuge. 15.These six cities shall be for refuge for the children of Israel, for the stranger, and for the sojourner among them, that anyone who kills a person accidentally may flee there.

16.But if he strikes him with an iron implement, so that he dies, he is a murderer; the murderer shall surely be put to death. 17.And if he strikes him with a stone in the hand, by which one could die, and he does die, he is a murderer; the murderer shall surely be put to death. 18. Or if he strikes him with a wooden hand weapon, by which one could die, and he does die, he is a murderer;

*the murderer shall surely be put to death. 19.The avenger of blood himself shall put the murderer to death; when he meets him, he shall put him to death. 20.If he pushes him out of hatred or, while lying in wait, hurls something at him so that he dies, 21.or in enmity he strikes him with his hand so that he dies, the one who struck him shall surely be put to death. He is a murderer. The avenger of blood shall put the murderer to death when he meets him.*

*22.However, if he pushes him suddenly without enmity, or throws something at him without lying in wait, 23.or uses a stone, by which a man could die, throwing it at him without seeing him, so that he dies, while he was not his enemy or seeking his harm, 24.then the congregation shall judge between the manslayer and the avenger of blood according to these judgments. 25.So the congregation shall deliver the manslayer from the hand of the avenger of blood, and the congregation shall return him to the city of refuge where he had fled, and he shall remain there until the death of the high priest who was anointed with the holy oil. 26.But if the manslayer at any time goes outside the limits of the city of refuge where he fled, 27. and the avenger of blood finds him outside the limits of his city of refuge, and the avenger of blood kills the manslayer, he shall not be guilty of blood. 28.because he should have remained in his city of refuge until the death of the high priest. But after the death of the high priest the manslayer may return to the land of his possession.*

*29.And these things shall be a statute of judgment to you throughout your generations in all your dwellings. 30.Whoever kills a person, the murderer shall be put to death on the testimony of witnesses; but one witness is not sufficient testimony against a person for the death penalty.*

*31.Moreover you shall take no ransom for the life of a murderer who is guilty of death, but he shall surely be put to death. 32.And you shall take no ransom for him who has fled to his city of refuge, that he may return to dwell in the land before the death of the priest. 33.So you shall not pollute the land where you are; for blood defiles the land, and no atonement can be made for the land, for the blood that is shed on it, except by the blood of him who shed it. 34.Therefore do not defile the land which you inhabit, in the midst of which I dwell; for I the Lord dwell among the children of Israel.'"*

## Chapter IV
## GOOD LAWS

We see that the laws established by God are good laws. This law concerning murder and manslaughter is followed today by Israel and most of the nations of the world. With the exception of the executioner (the avenger of blood) being the next of kin. The state assigns the executioner.

This is also a common sense law. The basics of it were established long before Moses. We find written on the Babylonian black obelisk found in the city of Susa and in four languages under the direction of Hammurabe, king of Babylon, the actual partial practice may have actually originated in the original Babylon under the founder of that first empire, Nimrod.

However, having been established detailed and confirmed by God Himself, through Moses to the new nation of Israel, it clearly established the standards for Israel, God's people.

Now, with the rules established we will follow the law.

We must keep our mind focused on God's original purpose for having chosen a special people. That is to bring the Messiah the promised Redeemer, to Adam, into the world. Two thousand years later Abraham and his children are chosen to be the channel to bring the messiah into the world. This fulfilled God's promise to Adam to provide a Redeemer for all mankind. This redemption to be individually received on the basis of faith only.* That is to cover the sin perpetuated by Satan to Adam and Eve in the Garden of Eden. The promise of a Redeemer is recorded this way in the Torah the book of Genesis. Let's read

Genesis 3; 14-15

> *14.So the LORD GOD said to the serpent:*
> "Because you have done this,
> you are cursed more than all
> cattle,
> And more than every beast of
> the field;

---

*Ref: Cain and Abel. Genesis 4;1-5

> On your belly you shall go,
> And you shall eat dust
> All the days of your life.
> 15. And I will put enmity
> Between you and the woman,
> And between your seed and
> her seed;
> He shall bruise your head,
> And you shall bruise His heel."

This may be difficult to understand, but let's try.

We must remember that we are all living under the curse pronounced upon us by God because of our physical parents, Adam and Eve, because of their disobedience. It is extended to us because we are all their offspring.

Now, the promise:

"He shall bruise your head, and you shall bruise His heel."

"He", is reference to the Messiah. In the book of the prophet Isaiah.

Isaiah 7; 14

*Therefore the Lord Himself will give you a sign: Behold, the virgin shall conceive and bear a son, and shall call His name Immanuel.*

Genesis 3 ; 15b

"And you shall bruise His heel."

This is referring to Satan's constant and continuous attempt to destroy the Messiah,

Jesus, which ended at the cross. Satan attempting to destroy physically or spiritually anyone connected with the lineage of the promised Messiah, the Jews.

Again from the prophet Isaiah.

I know that in the Tanach chapter 53 of Isaiah is forbidden reading among some Jewish congregations but read it you must, because without chapter 53, chapter 54 and it's blessings to the Jews have little meaning. Here is a clear description of what to look for in the promised Messiah.

Chapter 53
*Who has believed our report?*
*And in whom has the arm of*
*the LORD been revealed?*

2 For He shall grow up before
  Him as a tender plant,
And as a root out of dry ground.
He has no form or comeliness;
And when we see Him,
There is no beauty that we
  should desire Him.
3 He is despised and rejected by
  men,
A man of sorrows and
  acquainted with grief.
And we hid, as it were, our
  faces from Him;
He was despised' and we did
  not redeem Him.

4 Surely He has borne our
  griefs
And carried our sorrows;

*Yet we esteemed Him
    stricken,
Smitten by God, and afflicted.
5 But He was wounded for our
    transgressions,
He was bruised for our
    iniquities;
The chastisement for our peace
    was upon Him,
And by His stripes we are
    healed.
6 All we like sheep have gone
    astray;
We have turned, every one, to
    his own way;
And the LORD has laid on Him
    the iniquity of us all.*

*7 He was oppressed and He was
    afflicted,*

*Yet He opened not His mouth;
He was led as a lamb to the slaughter,
And as a sheep before its shearers is silent,
So He opened not His mouth.
8 He was taken from prison and from judgment,
And who will declare His generation?
For He was cut off from the land of the living;
For the transgressions of My people He was stricken.
9 And they made His grave with the wicked -
But with the rich at His death,
Because He had done no violence,*

*Nor was any deceit in His mouth.*

*10 Yet it pleased the Lord to bruise Him;*
*He has put Him to grief,*
*When you make His soul an offering for sin,*
*He shall see His seed, he shall prolong His days,*
*And the pleasure of the Lord shall prosper in His hand.*
*11 He shall see the labor of His soul, and be satisfied,*
*By His knowledge My righteous Servant shall justify many\*,*

---

\*"shall justify many", NOT ALL. Are you among the many?

*For He shall bear their
iniquities,*
*12 Therefore I will divide Him a
portion with the great,
And He shall divide the
spoil with the strong,
Because He poured out His
soul unto death,
And He was numbered with
the transgressors,
And He bore the sin of many,*
And made intercession for the
transgressors.

Yeshua of Nazareth has fulfilled every detail of this prophesy. For those who receive Him as their Messiah shall receive the promise of chapter 53 and 54.

Chapter 54

"Sing, O barren,
You who have not borne!
Break forth into singing, and cry
aloud,
You who have not labored with
child!
For more are the children of the
desolate
Than the children of the married
woman," says the Lord.
2 "Enlarge the place of your
tent,
And let them stretch out the
curtains of your dwellings;
Do not spare;
Lengthen your cords,
And strengthen your stakes,
3 For you shall expand to the

right and to the left,
And your descendants will
inherit the nations,
And make the desolate cities
inhabited.
4 "Do not fear, for you will not be
ashamed;
Neither be disgraced, for you
will not be put to shame;
For you will forget the shame
of your youth,
And will not remember the
reproach of your widowhood
anymore,
5 For your Maker is your
husband,
The LORD of hosts is His
name;
And your Redeemer is the Holy

*One of Israel;*
*He is called the God of the whole earth.*
*6 For the Lord has called you Like a woman forsaken and grieved in spirit, Like a youthful wife when you were refused,"*
*Says your God.*
*7 "For a mere moment I have forsaken you, But with great mercies I will gather you.*
*8 With a little wrath I hid My face from you in a moment; But with everlasting kindness I will have mercy on you."*
*Says the LORD, your Redeemer.*

9 *"For this is like the waters of*
   *Noah to Me;*
*For as I have sworn*
*That the waters of Noah would*
   *no longer cover the earth,*
*So have I sworn*
*That I would not be angry with*
   *you, nor rebuke you.*
*10 For the mountains shall depart*
*And the hills be removed,*
*But My kindness shall not*
   *depart from you,*
*Nor shall My covenant of peace*
   *be removed",*
*Says the LORD, who has mercy*
   *on you.*

*11 "O you afflicted one,*
*Tossed with tempest, and not*

comforted,
Behold, I will lay your stones
with colorful gems,
And lay your foundations with
sapphires.
12 I will make your pinnacles of
rubies,
Your gates of crystal,
And all your walls of precious
stones.
13 All your children shall be
taught by the Lord,
And great shall be the peace
of your children.
14 In righteousness you shall be
established;
You shall be far from
oppression, for you shall not
fear;

*And from terror, for it shall not
come near you.
15 Indeed they shall surely
assemble, but not because of
Me.
Whoever assembles against you
shall fall for your sake.*

*16 "Behold, I have created the
blacksmith
Who blows the coals in the fire,
Who brings forth an instrument
for his work;
And I have created the
spoiler to destroy.
17 No weapon formed against you
shall prosper,
And every tongue which rises
against you in judgment*

*You shall condemn,
This is the heritage of the
 servant of the LORD,
And their righteousness is from
Me,"
Says the Lord.*

Look again at 53:11. Do you see the Messiah removing your sins from you? And in verse 12: do you see the Messiah's death? The Messiah's death because the death penalty was the penalty pronounced upon Adam and Eve for their disobedience.

But don't despair, the death of Messiah was absolutely necessary to satisfy God's law. Isaiah 53:6. All we like sheep have gone astray. We have turned everyone to his own

way; and the Lord has laid on Him (the Messiah) the iniquity of us all.
But the Messiah liveth.

Go get your Tanach (Bible) and look up Isaiah 9 : 6 - 7.

> 6 *For unto us a Child is born,*
> *Unto us a Son is given;*
> *And the government will be*
>   *upon His shoulder.*
> *And His name will be called*
> *Wonderful, Counselor*
>   *Mighty God,*
> *Everlasting Father, Prince of*
>   *Peace.*
> *7 Of the increase of His*
>   *government and peace*
> *There will be no end,*
> *Upon the throne of David and*

*over His kingdom,
To order it and establish it with
judgment and justice
From that time forward, even
forever.
The zeal of the LORD of hosts
will perform this.*

Did God have a son? Hurry, read Proverbs 30:4.

*4 Who has ascended into heaven,
or descended?
Who has gathered the wind in
His fists?
Who has bound the waters in a
garment?
Who has established all the ends
of the earth?
What is His name, and what is*

*His Son's name,
If you know?*

Was the Son of God born of a Virgin? Hurry, hurry up and read Isaiah 7:14.

*14 Therefore the Lord Himself will give you a sign; Behold, the virgin shall conceive and bear a Son, and shall call His name Immanuel.*

If God had a Son, then His Son is God. If His Son is God, He has power over death. If the Son of God paid the death penalty for the sins of mankind He also has the power to be resurrected from the dead. God is God and the Messiah is alive and well.

What love that God would rescue us from that serpent, Satan, and the folly of Adam and Eve, our physical father and mother.

Paul, that wonderful Jewish scholar and author, was a star pupil under the great Jewish Biblical scholar, Gamaliel. Paul wrote in the book of Romans 14:9

> 9 For to this end Christ died and rose and lived again, that He might be Lord of both the dead and the living.

John, another writer and author of eternal fame wrote about Messiah in his book of Revelation 1:18a

> "I am He who lives, and was dead, and behold, I am alive forevermore. Amen."

When Yeshua accended into heaven after His resurrection he assumed his title of Melchezedek, the Great High Priest, without beginning, without end, no mother or father.

With that in mind, let's get back to the Holocaust. Why? Why, God? Why?

# CHAPTER V
# IS YESHUA THE MESSIAH?

This is a question that must be answered. The correct answer to this question involves the forgiveness of our sins and our resurrection and eternal life in the Heavens with our God and our Savior, the Messiah. We will answer this question from only one perspective, the Jewish Holocaust.

In Numbers chapter 35 we read from the Word of God about the manslayer, the murderer. The one who commits the crime. It was necessary for a court trial to take place to determine if the crime was pre-meditated murder or accidental. If accidental, it would have made the death a crime of manslaughter, second degree murder.

Let us take the well-recorded details of the world's most famous execution. We will follow it through from beginning to wherever it takes us, according to all available evidence recorded by the Jews in the Gospels and prophesies by the Jewish Prophets.

Was the death of Yeshua, the son of Mary and legal son of Joseph, outright murder or manslaughter?

In the Gospel of Luke it is recorded in Chapter 1 verses 26 to 35 ;

*26 Now in the sixth month the angel Gabriel was sent by God to a city of Galilee named Nazareth, 27 to a virgin betrothed to a man whose name was Joseph, of the house of David. The virgin's name was Mary.*

*28 And having come in, the angel said to her, "Rejoice, highly favored one, the Lord is with you; blessed are you among women!"*

*29 But when she saw him, she was troubled at his saying, and considered what manner of greeting this was. 30 Then the angel said to her, "Do not be afraid, Mary, for you have found favor with God. 31 And behold, you will conceive in your womb and bring forth a Son, and shall call His name JESUS. 32 He will be great and will be called the Son of the Highest; and the Lord God will give Him the throne of His father David. 33 And He will reign over the house of Jacob forever, and of His kingdom there will be no end."*

*34 Then Mary said to the angel, "How can this be, since I do not know a man?"*

*35 And the angel answered and said to her, "The Holy Spirit will come upon you, and the power of the Highest will overshadow you; therefore also, that Holy One who is to be born will be called the Son of God."*

Did God have a Son? Remember in the Tanach, The book of Proverbs;
Proverbs 30:4.

*"Who has ascended into heaven,*
  *or descended?*
*Who has gathered the wind in*
  *his fists?*

*Who has bound the waters in a
  garment?
Who has established all the ends
  of the earth?
What is His name, and what is
  His Son's name,
If you know?*

And just for good measure, please read from the Tanach
Isaiah 9:6
> *For unto us a Child is born,
> Unto us a Son is given;
> And the government will be
>   upon His shoulder.
> And His name will be called
> Wonderful, Counselor,
>   Mighty God.
> Everlasting Father, Prince of
>   Peace.*

In Jesus' day, there were many Jews in Israel who believed that Jesus was the Messiah.

The claim of Yeshua as the Son of God is very well established in both the Tanach and in the Gospels of the New Testament and followers of Yeshua the Messiah were careful to record this in detail.

## CHAPTER VI
## WHO KILLED YESHUA?

The Passover, about 30 A.D. It was, no doubt, a beautiful spring day.

John's Gospel records it this way: John 12:12 -15

*12 The next day a great multitude that had come to the feast, when they heard that Jesus was coming to Jerusalem, 13 took branches of palm trees and went out to meet Him, and cried out :*

*"Hosanna!*
*'Blessed is He who comes*

in the name of Lord!

The King of Israel!'

14 Then Jesus, when He had found a young donkey, sat on it; as it is written:

15   Fear not, daughter of Zion;
     Behold, Your King is coming,
     Sitting on a donkey's colt."

John 12:16-34:

16 His disciples did not understand these things at first; but when Jesus was glorified, then they remembered that these things were written about Him and that they had done these things to Him.

17 Therefore the people, who were with Him when He called Lazarus out of his tomb and raised him from

*the dead, bore witness. 18 For this reason the people also met Him, because they heard that He had done this sign.*

*19 The Pharisees therefore said among themselves, "You see that you are accomplishing nothing, Look, the world has gone after Him!"*

*20 Now there were certain Greeks among those who came up to worship at the feast. 21 Then they came to Philip, who was from Bethsaida of Galilee, and asked him, saying, "Sir, we wish to see Jesus."*

*22 Philip came and told Andrew, and in turn Andrew and Philip told Jesus.*

*23 But Jesus answered them, saying, "The hour has come that the Son of Man should be glorified. 24 Most assuredly, I say to you, unless a grain of wheat falls into the ground and dies, it remains alone; but if it dies, it produces much grain. 25 He who loves his life will lose it, and he who hates his life in this world will keep it for eternal life. 26 If anyone serves Me, let him follow Me; and where I am. there My servant will be also. If anyone serves Me, him My Father will honor.*

*27 Now My soul is troubled, and what shall I say? 'Father, save Me from this hour'? But for this purpose I came to this hour. 28 Father, glorify Your name."*

*Then a voice came from heaven, saying, "I have both glorified it and will glorify it again."*

*29 Therefore the people who stood by and heard it said that it had thundered. Others said, "An angel has spoken to Him."*

*30 Jesus answered and said, "This voice did not come because of Me, but for your sake. 31 Now is the judgment of this world; now the ruler of this world will be cast out. 32 And I, if I am lifted up from the earth, will draw all people to Myself."*

*33 This He said, signifying by what death He would die.*

*34 The people answered Him, "We have heard from the law that the Christ remains forever; and how can* you say, 'The Son of Man must be lifted up'? Who is this Son of Man?'

Psalm 89 : 36 - 37 ;
*36 His seed shall endure forever,
And His throne as the sun before Me;
37 It shall be established forever like the moon,
Even like the faithful witness in the sky.*

John 12 : 35 - 38 ;
*35 Then Jesus said to them, "A little while longer the light is with you. Walk while you have the light, lest darkness overtake you; he who walks in darkness does not know where he is going. 36 While you*

*have the light, believe in the light, that you may become sons of light."*

*These things Jesus spoke, and departed, and was hidden from them.*

*37 But although He had done so many signs before them, they did not believe in Him, 38 that the word of Isaiah the prophet might be fulfilled, which he spoke:*

> *"Lord, who has believed our report?*
> *And to whom has the arm of the LORD been revealed?"*

The details of the arrest and trial of Yeshua. This is extremely important.

John chapters 18 and 19 : 1 - 16 ;

*When Jesus had spoken these words, He went out with His disciples over the Brook Kidron, where there is a garden, which He and His disciples entered. 2. And Judas, who betrayed Him, also knew the place; for Jesus often met there with His disciples, 3. Then Judas, having received a detachment of troops, and officers from the chief priests and Pharisees, came there with lanterns, torches, and weapons. 4. Jesus therefore, knowing all things that would come upon Him, went forward and said to them, "Whom are you seeking?"*

*5. They answered Him, "Jesus of Nazareth.*

Jesus said to them, "I am He." And Judas, who betrayed Him, also stood with them. 6. Now when He said to them, "I am He." they drew back and fell to the ground.

7. Then He asked them again, "Whom are you seeking?"

And Jesus answered, "I have told you that I am He. Therefore, if you seek Me, let these go their way." that the saying might be fulfilled which He spoke, "Of those whom You gave Me I have lost none."

10. Then Simon Peter, having a sword, drew it and struck the high priest's servant, and cut off his right ear. The servant's name was Malchus.

11. So Jesus said to Peter, "Put

your sword into the sheath. Shall I not drink the cup which My Father has given Me?'

12. Then the detachment of troops and the captain and the officers of the Jews arrested Jesus and bound Him. 13. And they led Him away to Annas first, for he was the father-in-law of Caiaphas who was the high priest that year. 14. Now it was Caiaphas who advised the Jews that it was expedient that one man should die for the people.

15. And Simon Peter followed Jesus, and so did another disciple. Now that disciple was known to the high priest, and went with Jesus into the courtyard of the high priest. 16. But Peter stood at the door outside.

*Then the other disciple, who was known to the high priest, went out and spoke to her who kept the door, and brought Peter in. 17. Then the servant girl who kept the door said to Peter, "You are also one of this Man's disciples, are you?"*

*He said, "I am not."*

*18. Now the servants and officers who had made a fire of coals stood there, for it was cold, and they warmed themselves. And Peter stood with them and warmed himself.*

*19. The high priest then asked Jesus about His disciples and His doctrine.*

*20. Jesus answered him, "I spoke openly to the world. I always taught in synagogues and in the temple, where the Jews always meet, and in secret I have said nothing, 21. Why do you ask Me? Ask those who have heard Me what I say to them. Indeed they know what I said."*

*22. And when He had said these things, one of the officers who stood by struck Jesus with the palm of his hand, saying, "Do You answer the high priest like that?"*

*23. Jesus answered him, "If I have spoken evil, bear witness of the evil; but if well, why do you strike Me?"*

*24. Then Annas sent Him bound to Caiaphas the high priest.*

*25. Now Simon Peter stood and warmed himself. Therefore they said to him, "You are not also one of His disciples, are you?"*

*He denied it and said, "I am not!"*

*26. One of the servants of the high priest, a relative of him whose ear Peter cut off, said, "Did I not see you in the garden with Him?' 27. Peter then denied again; and immediately a rooster crowed.*

*28. Then they led Jesus from Caiaphas to the Praetorium, and it was early morning. But they themselves do not go into the Praetorium, lest they should be defiled, but that they might eat the Passover. 29. Pilate then went out to them and said, "What accusation do you bring against this Man?"*

*30. They answered and said to him. "If He were not an evildoer, we would not have delivered Him up to you."*

*31. Then Pilate said to them, "You take Him and judge Him according to your law."*

*Therefore the Jews said to him, "It is not lawful for us to put anyone to death," 32. that saying of Jesus might be fulfilled which He spoke, signifying by what death He would die.*

*33. Then Pilate entered the Praetorium again, called Jesus, and said to Him, "Are You the King of the Jews?"*

*34. Jesus answered him, "Are you speaking for yourself about this, or did others tell you this concerning Me?"*

*35. Pilate answered, "Am I a Jew? Your own nation and the chief priests have delivered You to me. What have you done?"*

*36. Jesus answered, "My kingdom is not of this world, If My kingdom were of this world My servants would fight, so that I should not be delivered to the Jews; but now My kingdom is not from here."*

*37. Pilate therefore said to Him, "Are You a king then?"*

*Jesus answered, "You say rightly that I am a king. For this cause I was born, and for this cause I have come into the world, that I should bear witness to the truth. Everyone who is of the truth hears My voice."*

*38. Pilate said to Him, "What is the*

*truth?" And when he had said this, he went out again to the Jews, and said to them, "I find no fault in Him at all.*

*39. But you have a custom that I should release someone to you at the Passover. Do you therefore want me to release to you the King of the Jews?"*

*40. Then they all cried again, saying, "Not this Man, but Barabbas!" Now Barabbas was a robber.*

*Chapter 19 - So then Pilate took Jesus and scourged Him. 2. And the soldiers twisted a crown of thorns and put it on His head, and they put on Him a purple robe. 3. They said, "Hail, King of the Jews!" And they struck Him with their hands.*

*4. Pilate then went out again, and said to them, "Behold, I am bringing Him out to you, that you may know that I find no fault in Him."*

*5. Then Jesus came out, wearing the crown of thorns and the purple robe. And Pilate said to them, "Behold the Man!"*

*6. Therefore, when the chief priests and officers saw Him, they cried out saying, "Crucify Him, crucify Him!"*

*Pilate said to them, "You take Him and crucify Him, for I find no fault in Him."*

*7. The Jews answered him, "We have a law, and according to our law He ought to die, because He* made Himself the Son of God."

8. Therefore, when Pilate heard that saying, he was the more afraid, 9. and went again to the Praetorium, and said to Jesus, "Where are you from?" But Jesus gave him no answer.

10. Then Pilate said to Him, "Are You not speaking to me? Do You not know that I have the power to crucify You, and power to release You?"

11. Jesus answered, "You could have no power at all against Me unless it had been given to you from above. Therefore the one who delivered Me to you has the greater sin."

12. From then on Pilate sought to

release Him, but the Jews cried out, saying, "If you let this Man go, you are not Caesar's friend. Whoever makes himself a king speaks against Caesar."

13. When Pilate therefore heard that saying, he brought Jesus out and sat down in the judgment seat in a place that is called The Pavement, but in Hebrew. Gabbatha.

14. Now it was the Preparation Day of the Passover, and about the sixth hour. And he said to the Jews, "Behold your King!"

15. But they cried out, "Away with Him, away with Him! Crucify Him!" Pilate said to them, "Shall I crucify your King?"

The chief priests answered, "We

*have no king but Caesar!"*

*16. Then he delivered Him to them to be crucified. Then they took Jesus and led Him away.*

In the Gospel of Matthew it is recorded this way by that great Jewish writer Matthew in ;

Matthew 27:23 -26

*23 Then the governor said, "Why, what evil has He done?"*

*But they cried out all the more, saying, "Let Him be crucified!"*

*24 When Pilate saw that he could not prevail at all, but rather that a tumult was raising, he took water and washed his hands before the multitude, saying, "I am innocent of the blood of this just Person. You see to it," And all the people answered and said, "His blood be on us and on our children."*

*26 Then he released Barabbas to them; and when he had scourged Jesus, he delivered Him to be crucified.*

THE CURSE - VERSE 25

And all the people answered and said, "*His blood be on us and our children."*

The chief priests and elders persuaded the multitude:

Verse 22 - Pilate said to them, *"What then shall I do with Jesus who is called Christ* (Messiah ?) *They all said to him, "Let Him be crucified. "*

The penalty phase imposed upon Jesus by the chief priests, elders and the Jewish multitude.

And so -" the Curse , *His blood, be on us and our children"* was placed on the Jews, by the Jews.

The CURSE has not yet been lifted. It is still there. The History of the Jews and Israel to this day shows that their self-imposed curse is still with them. And the condemnation is also still in effect.

However, the CURSE would not apply to that remnant of Jews who were followers and knew and believed that Jeshua was the Messiah and received Him as their Messiah. They and their children would be exempt from the CURSE.

Let's look again at the law. Who killed Jesus? The Romans or the Jews?

## Chapter VII
## 1st OR 2nd DEGREE MURDER

Numbers chapter 35 is the standard in the laws of God. The same principles of law on murder and manslaughter that are followed in most all the countries of the world today.

Let's see how they apply to the crucifixion of Yeshua, the Messiah.

It is very important in any trial to establish if the killing of a person is willful, pre-determined planned murder or that other contributing factors may have been significant in the mental process of driving a person or persons to kill someone.

Again, let's look to the detail records that we have in the Gospels of Yeshua, the Messiah. Also remember we read in Numbers 35 that we must have the indisputable evidence of two reliable witnesses.

We have the testimony of two very reliable witnesses.

One, a Pharisee who possibly approved of the action of the chief priests, elders and multitude; is none other than Saul, whose name became Paul after he came to realize that Yeshua was indeed the Messiah.

Paul writes in his first letter to the Corinthian believers:

Ist Corinthians 2:6-8

> *6 - However, we speak wisdom among those who are mature, yet not the wisdom of this age, nor of the rulers of this age, who are coming to nothing. 7 - But we speak the wisdom of God in a mystery, the hidden wisdom which God ordained before the ages for our glory, 8 - which none of the rulers of this age knew; for had they known, they would not have crucified the Lord of Glory.*

Wow! What a witness. None other than Paul the master Jewish scholar and an apostle of Yeshua the Messiah. Paul clearly states here that "Had they known" they would not have crucified the Lord of Glory.

Paul clearly puts the action of the Priests, Pharisees and the people in the category of second degree murder.

We need two indisputable witnesses. Who is the second witness?

How about Yeshua himself. The very victim of the crime.

Let's look at the record we have from another wonderful author who recorded the events of the crucifixion, Luke.

Luke was not a Jew. He was a Gentile and a physician by profession.

Luke records in the Gospel of Luke and quotes Yeshua as saying, while on the cross

Luke 23 : 34

> Then Jesus said "Father forgive them, for they do not know what they do."

Wow! Yeshua, the very victim of the crucifixion clearly states "they know not what they do."

So now we have it from two reliable and indisputable witnesses that the murder of Yeshua was 2nd degree murder. A murder committed out of rage.

Luke further states in the book of :
Acts 3 : 17 - 25 ;

> *17 Yet now, brethren, I know that you did it in ignorance, as did also your rulers. 18 But those things*

*which God foretold by the mouth of all His prophets, that the Christ* (Messiah) *would suffer. He has thus fulfilled.* 19 *Repent therefore and be converted, that your sins may be blotted out, so that times of refreshing may come from the presence of the Lord,* 20 *and that He may send Jesus Christ (*Yeshua Messiah), *who was preached to you before,* 21 *whom heaven must receive until the times of restoration of all things, which God has spoken by the mouth of His holy prophets since the world began.* 22 *For Moses truly said to the fathers,* (Deuteronomy 18:15) *'The Lord your God will raise up for you a Prophet like me from your brethren,*

*Him you shall hear in all things, whatever He says to you, 23 And it shall be that <u>every soul who will not hear that prophet shall be utterly destroyed from among the people.</u>' 24 Yes and all the prophets, from Samuel and those who follow, as many who have spoken, have also foretold these days, 25 You are sons of prophets, and of the covenant which God made with our fathers, saying to Abraham, 'And in your seed all the families of the earth shall be blessed.' To you first, God, having raised up His Servant Jesus, (Yeshua) sent Him to bless you, in turning away every one of you from your iniquities.'*

This is powerful stuff.

## Chapter VIII
## MELCHIZEDEK

Now that we have established that the murder of Yeshua Messiah was 2nd degree murder. The Law must be followed. The Jews who rejected their Messiah, Yeshua, placed a curse on themselves and their children, they are required to be assigned to the cities of refuge, for safety from the Avenger of Blood until the death of the High Priest.

Now, who is the high priest? Scripture records that Caiaphas was the high priest at the trial of Yeshua, and surely he was. But upon the death and then the resurrection and ascension of Yeshua, Yeshua assumed His position of Great High Priest after the order of Melchizedek. He is presently sitting at the right hand of God.

Mark 14 : 61b - 62 ;

61b *Again the high priest asked Him, saying to Him, "Are You the Christ, the Son of the Blessed?"*

62 *Jesus said, "I am. And you will see the Son of Man sitting at the right hand of the Power, and coming with the clouds of heaven."*

Hebrews 5:5,6

5 *So also Christ* (Yeshua) *did not glorify Himself to become High Priest. but it was He who said to Him:* (Yeshua)

*"You are My Son,*
*Today I have begotten you"*

6 As He also says in another place:

*"You are a priest forever*
*According to the order of*
*Melchizedek:;*

As He also says in another place in the tanach;
Psalm 110:4
*The LORD has sworn*
*And will not relent,*
*"You are a priest forever*
*According to the order of*
*Melchizedek."*

Genesis 14 : 18

*18 Then Melchizedek king of Salem (now Jerusalem) brought out bread and wine; he was the priest of God Most High.*

Hebrew 7:1 - 3 ;

*1 For this Melchizedek, king of Salem, priest of the Most High God, who met Abraham returning from the slaughter of the kings and blessed him, 2 to whom also Abraham gave a tenth part of all, first being translated "king of righteousness"* (holiness) *and then also king of Salem, meaning "king of peace" 3 without father, without mother, without genealogy, having neither beginning of days nor end of life, but made like the Son of*

*God, remains a priest continually.*

Hebrews 6: 19, 20 ;

*19 This hope we have as an anchor of the soul, both sure and steadfast, and which enters the Presence behind the veil, 20 where the forerunner has entered for us, even Jesus(Yeshua Messiah) having become High Priest forever according to the order of Melchezedek.*

Because the priest, the scribes and the people placed a curse upon themselves. "Let his blood be upon us and our children". That CURSE is still in effect today. It has not yet been lifted. And according to God's law the

Jews were to flee to the cities of refuge. Three cities designated on the east side of the Jordan and three cities designated on the west side of the Jordan river.

They have not. They never have.

Therefore, it is the responsibility of the next of kin to chase down those responsible for the murder of Yeshua Messiah so long as they are not in their safe haven, a designated city of refuge until the high priest dies.

But now Yeshua became High Priest at His accession into heaven and will never die. The Jews have been scattered all over the world from the time of the crucifixion of their Messiah, Yeshua.

The major scattering beginning in A.D. 70 with the total destruction of Jerusalem at the hands of the Romans.

The avenger of blood, the next of kin, Yeshua had four brothers and several sisters. Two of his brothers we know were active in the Jewish Christian Synagogue. James was the pastor and Jude who wrote the book of Jude. Two other brothers, Simon and Joseph, we don't have any record of their activities.

According to Clarence Larkin, in his book Dispensational Truth page 137 he states that the family of Yeshua was traceable to A.D. 324. I'm sure that there are descendants still alive today and still have the legal responsibility to execute the law. Which must be executed until the High Priest dies.

But ------ the Jews rejected their Messiah, Yeshua (Jesus the Christ), The High Priest. Yeshua Messiah (Jesus the Christ) at His accession into Heaven assumed His title and position as Great High Priest after the order of Melchizedek. No mother, no father, no beginning, no ending. This Melchizedek Great High Priest of God shall never die.

These dear Jewish souls have been wandering from city to city establishing ghettos, maintaining their identity, wandering from country to country for 2,000 years. Moses prophesied in:

Deuteronomy 28: 64-67

*64 Then the LORD will scatter you*

among all peoples, from one end of the earth to the other, and there you shall serve other gods, which neither you nor your fathers have known - wood and stone, 65 And among those nations you shall find no rest, <u>nor shall the sole of your foot have a resting place</u>; but there the LORD will give you a trembling heart, failing eyes, and anguish of soul. 66 Your life shall hang in doubt before you; you shall fear day and night, and have no assurance of life. 67 In the morning you shall say' 'Oh, that it were evening!' And at the evening you shall say, 'Oh, that it were morning!' because of the fear which terrifies your heart and because of the sight which your eyes see.

The Jews started returning to the land in the late 1890's with the beginning of the Zionist movement.

In 1917 the British General Allenby arranged to declare Palestine a homeland for the Jews.

In 1948 the Jews gained a foot hold in Palestine and declared the State of Israel. The wars to maintain their presence in Palestine are still being fought in a bloody war today.

Why? Because the Jewish people have returned to the land before the death of the high priest and are still under the CURSE.   See again :
Numbers 35: 32:

*32 And you shall take no ransom for him who has fled to his city of refuge, that he may return to dwell in the land before the death of the priest.*

The Jews have returned to the promised land too soon, and not in the will of God.

OH! My dear Jewish friends. the Great High Priest Melchezedek (Yeshua, Messiah) will never die. How, now, can you be free from the terrible CURSE? And from being chased all over the earth and even in Israel and Jerusalem trying to escape the execution? How can you be free from the Holocausts? Yes, even from the holocausts taking place in the very land of Israel today.

The Avenger of blood is still chasing the Jews. There are parts of bodies of your families splattered over buildings, people and vehicles for the whole world to witness in the very promised land today. The blood is still flowing because the land has been defiled.

> We read in Numbers 35 : 33 ;
> *So you shall not pollute the land where you are; for blood defiles the land, and no atonement can be made for the land, for the blood that is shed on it, except by the blood of him who shed it.*

When the Jews crucified Yeshua, their Messiah, they defiled the land. The atonement for the land can only be made by the blood of him who shed it.

Here it is, 1st John 1 : 7b ;

*and the blood of Jesus Christ His Son cleanses us from all sin.*

My dear Jewish friends, there is light at the end of the tunnel. It's not too late for Israel. There is a way out.

You can receive Yeshua your Savior and proclaim Him King of Israel.

## Chapter IX
## THE KING IS COMING

Around A.D. 30 when Yeshua rode into Jerusalem for the Passover on a foal of a donkey and :

Mark 11 : 9 , 10 ;
    9 Then those who went before and those who followed cried out saying:
"Hosanna!
Blessed is He who comes in the
  name of the Lord!
10 Blessed is the kingdom of our
  father David
That comes in the name of the
  Lord!
Hosanna in the highest!"

When Yeshua Messiah entered Jerusalem he was proclaimed King of Israel.

Matthew 21: 4 , 5 ;
> 4 All this was done that it might be fulfilled which was spoken by the prophet, saying:
> 5 "Tell the daughter of Zion,
> 'Behold your King is coming to you,
> Lowly, and sitting on a donkey,
> A colt, the foal of a donkey.'"

Please read with me from the Prophet, Zacheriah 9:9
> 9 Rejoice greatly. O daughter of Zion!
> Shout, O daughter of Jerusalem!

*Behold your King is coming*
*to you;*
*He is just and having salvation,,*
*Lowly and riding on a donkey,*
*A colt, the foal of a donkey.*

Yeshua entered Jerusalem and was proclaimed King. But was soon rejected by the priests, scribes and people and they began the process of his trial.

At the crucifixion of Yeshua Messiah the clock stopped for the Jews. It was the end of the prophet Daniel's 69th week of the 70 weeks that he proclaimed. There is still one week to go for the Jews. Or one day is as a year, 7 years to go.

In the meantime God has been

reaching out to the Gentiles. For almost 2,000 years now, starting with the Jewish believers in Jerusalem and spreading His Gospel, starting in Jerusalem and going throughout the world through many generations.

Most Gentiles have also rejected Jesus the Messiah as their Savior. Although there have been many who have received Jesus as their Messiah and Savior and have been a constant witness throughout the generations.

When Daniel's 70th week begins, which may be very soon, it will again be God's time for the Jews. Before the 70th week closes the Jews, in mass, will proclaim Yeshua their King and then, and only then, will God place the crown on the head of His Son Jeshua and proclaim Him King of Kings and Lord of Lords.

Now - What about the Jews? The High Priest, Melchezedek is still alive and well. How can the Jews be free from the curse their fathers placed on them? By proclaiming Yeshua as their Messiah and King of Israel.

King Yeshua has the full right and authority to pardon. Yeshua King of Israel will fully pardon all the Jews who accept Him and commit themselves to Him who is also Melchezedek most High Priest of God.

OH! What a day of rejoicing that will be in Jerusalem.

But wait - there's more.

## Chapter X
## WHAT ABOUT THE GENTILES?

A remnant of Jewish believers brought the Gospel of Yeshua the Messiah (Jesus the Christ) to the gentile world. And truly God's promise to Abraham that the Jews would be a blessing to all the Nations of the world has come true. The early Jewish believers that Yeshua is Messiah, faithful to the command of Jesus, went into all the world and preached the Gospel. Today there is not one nation on earth that has not heard about the saving love of Jesus Christ, Yeshua the Messiah, God Himself. He became the perfect acceptable and final sacrifice for all who receive him as their personal sacrifice to God for the forgiveness of their sins.

But - now, we can very clearly see that God has allowed many devastating Holocausts, where many millions of Jews have perished, under devastating conditions, because they rejected Him, their Messiah Yeshua (Jesus Christ).

Can you possibly imagine in your mind what is going to happen to the Gentiles who also reject Jesus Christ to be their Messiah and Savior?

There are more Holocausts to come. With the destruction of the World Trade Center Twin Towers* and the Pentagon etc., it may be just the beginning. If not, expect it. There will be far greater holocausts than the world has yet seen.

---

*Isaiah 33 : 18 and 19

The only government that will be successful in the nation of Israel is a monarchy with Yeshua Messiah sitting on the throne of David as Lord of Lords and King of Kings. And this can only happen when the Jews proclaim Him their Messiah and King, Only the King has the power to pardon. As king Yeshua who is also the Great High Priest after the order of Melchizedek who will never die, will joyfully pardon as King his people the Jews who proclaim Him King.

God, through the prophet Isaiah prophesied ;
Isaiah 9 : 6 , 7 ;

*6 For unto us a Child is born,*
*unto us a Son is given;*
*And the government will be*
*upon His shoulder.*
*And His name will be called*

*Wonderful, Counselor,*
*Mighty God,*
*Everlasting Father, Prince of Peace.*
*7 Of the increase of His government and peace*
*There will be no end,*
*Upon the throne of David and over His kingdom,*
*To order it and establish it with judgment and justice*
*From that time forward, even forever.*
*The zeal of the Lord of hosts will perform this.*

Jew, Gentile, what are you going to do? Jesus your Savior, Yeshua your Messiah, shows his love for you. Are you going to reject Him like the Jews did at the crucifixion? Or are you going to accept His salvation and commit your life to Him?

John 3 : 16 ;

> For God so loved the world that He gave His only begotten Son, that whoever believes in Him should not perish but have everlasting life.

Our wonderful Jewish teacher, Paul shares this with us in his book to the believers in Rome.

Romans 10 : 1 - 21 ;

> Brethren, my heart's desire and prayer to God for Israel is that they may be saved. 2. For I bear them witness that they have a zeal for

*God, but not according to knowledge. 3. For they being ignorant of God's righteousness, and seeking to establish their own righteousness, have not submitted to the righteousness of God. 4. For Christ is the end of the law for righteousness to everyone who believes.*

*5. For Moses writes about the righteousness which is of the law, "The man who does those things shall live by them." 6. But the righteousness of faith speaks in this way, "Do not say in your heart, 'Who will ascend into heaven?'" (that is, to bring Christ down from above) 7. or, "'Who will descend into the abyss?'" (that is, to bring Christ up from the dead).  8. But what does it say? "The word is near you, in your mouth and in your heart" (that is, the word of faith which we preach): 9. that if you confess with your mouth the Lord Jesus and believes in your heart that God has raised Him from the dead, you will be saved.  10. For with the heart one believes unto righteousness, and with the mouth confession is made unto salvation. 11. For the Scripture says, "Whoever believes on Him will not be put to shame."  12. For there is no distinction between Jew and Greek, for the same Lord over all is rich to all who call upon Him.  13. For "whoever calls on the name of the LORD shall be saved."*

*14. How then shall they call on Him in whom they have not believed? And how shall they believe in Him of whom they have not heard? And how shall they hear without a preacher? 15. And how shall they preach unless they are sent? As it is written:*

> *"How beautiful are the feet of those who preach the gospel of peace,*
> *Who bring glad tidings of good things!"*

*14. But they have not all obeyed the gospel. For Isaiah says, "Lord,* who has believed our report?" 17. So then faith comes by hearing, and hearing by the word of God.

18. But I say, have they not heard? Yes indeed:
> "Their sound has gone out to all the earth,
> And their words to the ends of the world."

19. But I say, did Israel not know? First Moses says:
> "I will provoke you to jealousy by those who are not a nation,
> I will move you to anger by a foolish nation."

20. But Isaiah is very bold and says:

> "I was found by those who did
> not seek Me;
> I was made manifest to those
> who did not ask for Me."

21. But to Israel he says:
> "All day long I have stretched
> out My hands
> To a disobedient and contrary
> people."

And again Paul, as an apostle of Jesus the Christ.

Ephesians 2 : 89 ;

8. For by grace you have been saved through faith, and that not of yourselves; it is the gift of God, 9.
not of works, lest anyone should boast.

My dear Jewish friends, let the God of Israel open your heart to His Messiah, Yeshua. In Yeshua you will find the true peace that you are searching for.

Hurry and make up your mind. You may yet just escape the great holocausts to come.

To the Schneiders, my dear neighbors in Jerusalem, who inspired me to search for the answers in the Tanach to the holocausts, thank you. The Lover of your soul is looking for you. Let Him know where you are, He loves you and wants you.

May the Love of Yeshua Messiah find his way into your hearts.

Shalom

## BIBLIOGRAPHY

All scriptures are quoted from the New King James translation of the Bible. Thomas Nelson Publishers London.

The Trail of Blood
    Ashland Ave. Baptist Church
    Lexington, Kentucky, Copyright 1931

Dispensational Truth (pages 136 and 137)
    Clarence Larkin Estate
    P.O. Box 334, Glenside, PA 19038 USA
    Copyrighted 1920

For Bible correspondence courses in any major language or for personal information please contact:

Bible Institute of Jerusalem
P.O. Box 174
Jerusalem, Israel 91001
TL/FX : 011-972-2-624-2572
e-mail : ega-bij@netmedia.net.il
web site : www.bibleinstitutjerusalem.edu

B.I.O.J has both long distance education and on campus classes in downtown Jerusalem, Israel. Class semesters run from September to December and January to June.